W9-BHG-540

CREATE IT!

EXPRESSIONIST ART

Alix Wood

 Gareth Stevens
PUBLISHING

Thank you to
Davina Cresswell
and Jemma Martin
for their help with
this book.

Please visit our website, **www.garethstevens.com**. For a free color catalog of all
our high-quality books, call toll free 1-800-542-2595 or fax 1-877-542-2596

Cataloging-in-Publication Data

Names: Wood, Alix.
Title: Expressionist art / Alix Wood.
Description: New York : Gareth Stevens Publishing, 2017. | Series: Create it! | Includes index.
Identifiers: ISBN 9781482450354 (pbk.) | ISBN 9781482450378 (library bound) |
    ISBN 9781482450361 (6 pack)
Subjects: LCSH: Expressionism (Art)--Juvenile literature. | Expressionism (Art)--Germany--Juvenile literature.
Classification: LCC N6494.E9 W66 2017| DDC 759.06'42--dc23

First Edition

Published in 2017 by
Gareth Stevens Publishing
111 East 14th Street, Suite 349
New York, NY 10003

Produced for Gareth Stevens by Alix Wood Books
Designed by Alix Wood
Editor: Eloise Macgregor

Photo credits: Cover, 1, 7, 8, 11, 13, 16 top and bottom, 17, 18 bottom, 19, 21, 22 bottom, 23, 25, 26, 27, 28 top, 29 © Alix
Wood; 3, 6, 16 middle, 28 bottom © Dollar Photo Club; 15 © The Detroit Institute of Arts; 18 top © Neftali/Shutterstock;
20 © Dreamstime; 21 top © Legacy 1995/Dreamstime; 24 Sergey Goryachev/Shutterstock; all remaining images are in
the public domain.

Printed in the United States of America
CPSIA compliance information: Batch #CS16GS: For further information
contact Gareth Stevens, New York, New York at 1-800-542-2595.

CONTENTS

WHAT IS EXPRESSIONIST ART?

Expressionist artists paint moods and ideas rather than just painting objects or scenery. They want their paintings to bring out emotions in the people who look at them. Expressionist artists often used swirling, swaying brushstrokes to make a painting appear moody.

Vincent Van Gogh's *Wheat Field with Crows* is an Expressionist painting. What emotions does this painting make you feel?

The First Expressionist?

Expressionism began in the early 1900s. However, this painting, *View of Toledo* by El Greco, was painted around 1600! It is very like modern expressionist paintings. El Greco's work may have influenced the later artists.

TECHNIQUE TIPS

What makes Van Gogh's wheat field seem moody? Is it the colors? Is it the violent brushstrokes, or the flock of black crows? The answer is probably a mixture of all of these.

COLORS AND MOODS

Sometimes we attach a color to the emotions we are feeling, such as "seeing red" or "feeling blue." Expressionist artists use color to create different moods. They can choose a bright or dull shade of each color, too. Color wheels, like the one below, can help artists choose what colors to use. Red, yellow, and blue are **primary colors**. All the other colors can be mixed by using them.

Complementary colors are opposite each other on the color wheel.

TECHNIQUE TIPS

Using colors next to each other on the wheel together makes a painting seem calm. Using colors that are opposite each other on the wheel makes a painting seem lively.

Try creating two very different moods in your art.

You will need: thin printer paper, markers

1 Using a black marker, draw a simple outline drawing. Trace your drawing so you have two that are exactly the same.

2 Color one drawing using colors next to each other on the color wheel. Color the other drawing using colors from opposite sides of the wheel.

calm and restful

lively and fun

VINCENT VAN GOGH

Vincent Van Gogh was a **Postimpressionist** artist, but he was also an Expressionist. He often used broad brushstrokes in his painting. In *The Starry Night* below, instead of accurately painting the sky, he painted his feelings about the universe, filled with whirling, exploding stars and galaxies. The village seems to huddle underneath the vast sky.

Van Gogh's *The Starry Night*

CREATE IT!

You will need: white chalk, paints,
a paintbrush, dark-colored paper

1 Draw an outline of
your picture using
white chalk.

2 Recreate Van Gogh's
brushstrokes using
your finger or a paintbrush
dipped in paint.

3 Make the
directions
of your brush
or finger strokes
follow the
swirling patterns
of Van Gogh's
painting.

Van Gogh liked to paint sunflowers. He painted the sunflowers during a period in his life when he was feeling happy. He was waiting for a visit from his artist friend, Paul Gauguin, and thought Gauguin would like their happy colors.

TECHNIQUE TIPS

Most artists place **contrasting** colors as a background in a painting. But Van Gogh put yellow flowers in a yellow vase on a yellow table instead.

CREATE IT!

You will need: colored paper, pastels or chalks, hairspray

1 Start drawing at the top of your paper, so the pastels don't smudge.

2 Draw some cheerful bright sunflowers.

3 Draw in your vase and tabletop. When you have finished, to keep the picture from smudging, ask an adult to spray your picture lightly with hairspray.

Most artists paint their **self-portrait** at some point. Van Gogh wanted to not just paint how he looked, but paint how he felt, too. How do you think he was feeling when he painted the self-portrait below?

Van Gogh painted over 40 self-portraits. This was one of his last. He gave the painting to his brother, Theo.

TECHNIQUE TIPS

Van Gogh had reddish hair. He used blue from the opposite side of the color wheel as his background. What color would you choose as a background for your portrait?

CREATE IT!

You will need: paper, poster paint, a thick paintbrush

1 Using a pencil, draw your head and shoulders. Think how you are feeling and make your eyes and mouth look sad or happy.

2 Choose your background color to match your mood. This purple seems like a sad color. It is a nice contrast to fair hair, too.

3 Paint your picture using thick swirls of paint. If you are painting a happy picture use happy, bright colors. This picture is sad so it is painted using **muted** colors.

FRANZ MARC

Franz Marc used colors to give meaning to his paintings. He thought blue was a male color, and **spiritual**. He believed yellow was female and full of joy. Marc used red when he wanted a violent color.

Marc often painted blue horses. In *Blue Horses 1*, he painted a simple, rounded outline of the horse. He **echoed** the same rounded shapes in his background.

Marc's painting *Animals in a Landscape* is also known as *Painting with Bulls.* Can you find three bulls?

TECHNIQUE TIPS

Marc used bold, bright colors in his paintings. Many of Marc's paintings were of animals. Marc believed animals were more natural and purer than people. He often painted the same animals in different colors in one painting. Each color **symbolized** a different emotion.

CREATE IT!

You will need: paper, a pencil, watercolor paints

1 Using pencil, draw several of the same animal on your paper. To make the drawing interesting, have them facing different directions, or have some standing and some lying down.

2 Divide your paper up into interesting shapes. Using a pencil, draw some curved lines all over the paper. Make sure some of the lines **overlap** your original drawing.

3 Choose which animal you want to look calm, and which you want to look angry. Color them in the colors you think best suits their mood. Color in your background.

4 Outline your animals in black marker.

EDVARD MUNCH

Edvard Munch's painting *The Scream* is probably the best-known Expressionist painting. Munch's red and orange colors and the frightened figure express anxiety and pain. He said that watching a blood-red sunset one evening made him tremble with fright. This event inspired him to paint *The Scream*.

A postage stamp showing Munch's famous painting *The Scream*.

You will need: chalks or pastels, black construction paper

1 Using white chalk, draw the outlines of your drawing onto some black paper.

2 Starting from the top of the paper, color in the picture. Pastels and chalks smudge so work carefully.

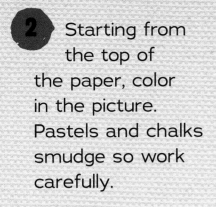

3 You can use your finger to blend the colors together.

MARC CHAGALL

Artist Marc Chagall was known for his dreamlike paintings. He liked to create art using his imagination and his memory. Born in Russia, Chagall moved to several different countries. Chagall missed his home town of Vitebsk. He often used memories of the town in his paintings. In many of his pictures, figures seem to float in the sky, as if they were looking down on his faraway home.

Chagall's dreamlike *Song of Solomon IV* (1958) shows David and Bathsheba on the back of a winged horse flying over Jerusalem.

CREATE IT!

You will need: pastels or chalks, colored paper

1 Think of a fun person or animal you could draw flying through the sky. Using a dark pastel or chalk, draw the outline of your dream idea.

2 Pastels and chalks smudge very easily. Always start coloring it in from the top of your picture, so your hand doesn't smudge your work.

3 You don't have to color things in their real colors. Remember this is a dream! Try using two different colors on top of each other. You can smudge them together to mix them.

In Chagall's dreamlike paintings, he often drew some of the objects or people upside down or on their sides. In his painting *I and the Village*, can you see a woman standing on her head?

CREATE IT!

You will need: a ruler, paper, a pencil, watercolors, a paintbrush

1 Make your own topsy-turvy painting. Using a ruler and pencil draw diagonal lines from the corners to divide the paper into four. Using pencil, draw a picture in one section. Turn the paper, and then draw a picture in another section. Repeat this until all four sections are filled.

2 Paint your picture. Pick colors that suit your dream. Wait for each section to dry before you turn and paint the next section. Otherwise, you may smudge the painting that you have already done.

3 Once your picture is finished you could turn it a different way up every day!

WASSILY KANDINSKY

Wassily Kandinsky was an **Abstract Expressionist** artist. His work gave the impression it was painted quickly and with emotion. He drew inspiration from music. You can't see music. Music can't represent people or landscapes. It can only suggest emotion and inspire your imagination. Kandinsky wanted to paint the emotions that music makes you feel.

TECHNIQUE TIPS

One day, Kandinsky entered his **studio** and looked in wonder at one of his paintings. He didn't recognize it, but thought the bright colors looked amazing. Then he realized it was one of his paintings turned on its side! From then on, he decided to give up painting real objects, and just paint colors.

This Kandinsky painting would look good any way up!

CREATE IT!

You will need: a piece of music in your head, paper, paints, a paintbrush

1 Think of a piece of music that you like. Just think of the tune and not any of the words, if it has them. How does the music make you feel?

2 Try to paint your music. Think what colors you might use. Would you need happy colors or sad colors? Should the paint be smooth or scattered brushstrokes?

This tune was *Happy Birthday!*

CREATE IT!

You will need: colored markers, paper, watercolor paint, paintbrush

1 Expressionist artists use lines to put feeling into their art. Practice drawing lines to show different moods. Choose colors that suit the mood, too.

angry

calm

happy

fun

organized

2 Create a background for your picture by drawing shapes using a black marker. Use straight lines, wavy lines, or both together. These lines will create a mood too, so think what mood you want each shape to be.

3 Fill in each shape with lines using a marker. In this picture the artist used calm lines and colors on the left-hand side.

4 Paint over the marker lines using watercolor. Choose colors that suit the mood of the lines underneath.

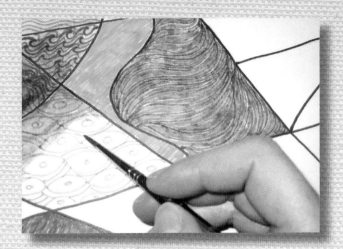

5 Continue to fill in all your shapes with marker lines. This artist used angry lines on the right-hand side. Paint over the shapes. You can leave some shapes unpainted if you like.

FRANZ KLINE

Franz Kline was an Abstract Expressionist artist who created large pieces using house paint and brushes. His best-known paintings were created using only black and white paint. He relied on his dramatic brushstrokes rather than color to make his paintings full of feeling.

TECHNIQUE TIPS

When you see black lines on a white background, it is easy to think the black shapes are the most important. Kline believed that the white shapes he created were just as valuable.

CREATE IT!

Paint a black and white portrait using big, bold brushstrokes.

You will need: poster paints, a wide paintbrush, thick paper or cardboard

1 Cover your paper in thick, white paint. Once the paint is dry, draw your face using thick, black paint.

2 Mix the black and white together to make gray. Use the gray to paint in some shadows.

GLOSSARY

Abstract Expressionist An art movement that combined Expressionist art with Abstract art.

complementary colors Colors which, when placed next to each other, create the strongest contrast.

contrasting Strikingly different.

echoed Repeated.

Expressionist An art movement that concentrated on emotional effect to evoke moods or ideas.

muted Toned down.

overlap To lie over something and partly cover it.

Postimpressionist A member of an art movement that came after the Impressionist movement but was influenced by them.

primary colors Colors from which all other colors may be made. In paint, primary colors are red, yellow, and blue (in light, they are red, green, and blue).

self-portrait A painting of oneself made by oneself.

spiritual Relating to the spirit, or to sacred or religious matters.

studio The working place of an artist.

symbolized Stood for something else.

FURTHER INFORMATION

Books
Brooks, Susie. *Get Into Art People: Enjoy Great Art-Then Create Your Own!* New York, NY: Kingfisher, 2013.

Cernak, Linda. *Vincent Van Gogh (World's Greatest Artists)*. North Mankato, MN: Child's World, 2014.

Websites
Ducksters site with information about famous Expressionist painters and their work:
http://www.ducksters.com/history/art/expressionism.php

National Gallery of Art website with fun downloadable abstract art program:
http://www.nga.gov/content/ngaweb/education/kids/kids-brushster.html

INDEX